Double Shell Stitch

Finished Size: Approximately 35½" x 48"

MATERIALS

Sport Weight Yarn, approximately:
 Main Color: 12 ounces, (340 grams, 1,500 yards)
 Color A: 3 ounces, (90 grams, 375 yards)
 Color B: 3 ounces, (90 grams, 375 yards)
 Crochet hook, size G (4.50 mm) **or** size needed for gauge

GAUGE: 3 Shells and 8½ rows = 4"

With Main Color, ch 158 **loosely**.
Row 1 (Right side)**:** Sc in second ch from hook, ★ skip next 2 chs, 7 dc in next ch **(Shell made)**, skip next 2 chs, sc in next ch; repeat from ★ across: 26 Shells.
Note: Loop a short piece of yarn around any stitch to mark last row as **right** side.

Row 2: Ch 3 (cou█
(YO, insert hook i█
through 2 loops o█
4 loops on hook, ⬚
hook in next st an█ █████ ████, YO and draw through
2 loops on hook) 7 times, YO and draw through all 8 loops
on hook *(Fig. 3, **Cluster made**)*, ch 3, sc in next dc, ch 3;
repeat from ★ across to last 4 sts, (YO, insert hook in next st
and pull up a loop, YO and draw through 2 loops on hook)
4 times, YO and draw through all 5 loops on hook.

Fig. 3

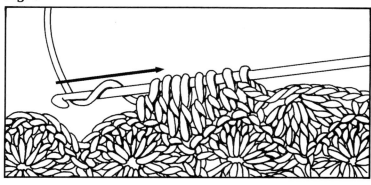

Row 3: Ch 3, turn; 3 dc in same st, sc in next sc, ★ work
Shell in next Cluster, sc in next sc; repeat from ★ across to
last st, 4 dc in last st.
Row 4: Ch 1, turn; sc in first dc, ★ ch 3, work Cluster, ch 3,
sc in next dc; repeat from ★ across.
Row 5: Ch 1, turn; sc in first sc, ★ work Shell in next
Cluster, sc in next sc; repeat from ★ across.
Note: Begin working in Stripe Sequence as follows:
2 rows Color A, 2 rows Main Color, 2 rows Color A,
6 rows Main Color, 2 rows Color B, 2 rows Main Color,
2 rows Color B, 6 rows Main Color. Repeat these 24 rows
throughout.
Rows 6-101: Repeat Rows 2-5, 24 times.
Edging: Working in end of rows, (5 dc, sc) in end of same
row, † skip next 2 rows, work Shell in sp before next row,
skip next 2 rows, (sc in sp before next row, skip next 2 rows,
work Shell in sp before next row, skip next 2 rows) across to
next corner †; working in free loops of beginning ch, (sc,
5 dc, sc) in first ch, skip next 2 chs, work Shell in next ch,
skip next 2 chs, (sc in next ch, skip next 2 chs, work Shell in
next ch, skip next 2 chs) across to last ch, (sc, 5 dc, sc) in
last ch; working in end of rows, repeat from † to † once, (sc,
5 dc) in end of last row, slip st in next sc; finish off.

ALUMINUM CROCHET HOOKS												
U.S.	B-1	C-2	D-3	E-4	F-5	G-6	H-8	I-9	J-10	K-10½	N	P	Q
Metric - mm	2.25	2.75	3.25	3.50	3.75	4.00	5.00	5.50	6.00	6.50	9.00	10.00	15.00

Fisherman

Finished Size: Approximately 38" x 51"

MATERIALS
Sport Weight Yarn, approximately:
   24 ounces, (680 grams, 2,400 yards)
Crochet hook, size G (4.50 mm) **or** size needed for gauge
Yarn needle

GAUGE: 16 dc and 10 rows = 4"

TWIST PANEL (Make 2)

Ch 15 **loosely**.

Row 1: Dc in fourth ch from hook and in each ch across: 13 sts.

Row 2 (Right side): Ch 3 **(counts as first dc, now and throughout)**, turn; work Front Post tr **(abbreviated FPtr)** around post of next dc **(Fig. 1, page 1)**, dc in next 3 dc, skip next dc, work FPtr around post of next dc, dc in same dc, work FPtr around post of same dc as last FPtr, skip next dc, dc in next 3 dc, work FPtr around post of next dc, dc in last dc.

Note: Loop a short piece of yarn around any stitch to mark last row as **right** side.

Row 3: Ch 3, turn; work Back Post tr **(abbreviated BPtr)** around post of next FPtr, dc in next 3 dc, work BPtr around post of next FPtr, dc in next dc, work BPtr around post of next FPtr, dc in next 3 dc, work BPtr around post of next FPtr, dc in last dc.

Row 4: Ch 3, turn; work FPtr around post of next BPtr, dc in next 3 dc, skip next 2 sts, work FPtr around post of next BPtr, working **behind** FPtr just worked, dc in skipped dc, working in **front** of FPtr, work FPtr around post of skipped BPtr, dc in next 3 dc, work FPtr around post of next BPtr, dc in last dc.

Repeat Rows 3 and 4 for pattern until Panel measures approximately 51", ending by working Row 4.
Finish off.

BOBBLE PANEL (Make 2)

Ch 25 **loosely**.

Row 1 (Right side): Dc in fourth ch from hook and in each ch across: 23 sts.

Note: Loop a short piece of yarn around any stitch to mark last row as **right** side.

Row 2: Ch 3 **(counts as first dc, now and throughout)**, turn; work Back Post dc **(abbreviated BPdc)** around post of next dc **(Fig. 1, page 1)**, sc in next dc, (tr in next dc, sc in next dc) across to last 2 dc, work BPdc around post of next dc, dc in last dc.

Row 3: Ch 3, turn; work Front Post dc **(abbreviated FPdc)** around post of next BPdc, sc in next sc, (tr in next tr, sc in next sc) across to last 2 sts, work FPdc around post of next BPdc, dc in last dc.

Row 4: Ch 3, turn; work BPdc around post of next FPdc, tr in next sc, (sc in next tr, tr in next sc) across to last 2 sts, work BPdc around post of next FPdc, dc in last dc.

Row 5: Ch 3, turn; work FPdc around post of next BPdc, tr in next tr, (sc in next sc, tr in next tr) across to last 2 sts, work FPdc around post of next BPdc, dc in last dc.

Row 6: Ch 3, turn; work BPdc around post of next FPdc, tr in next tr, (sc in next sc, tr in next tr) across to last 2 sts, work BPdc around post of next FPdc, dc in last dc.

Row 7: Ch 3, turn; work FPdc around post of next BPdc, sc in next tr, (tr in next sc, sc in next tr) across to last 2 sts, work FPdc around post of next BPdc, dc in last dc.

Row 8: Ch 3, turn; work BPdc around post of next FPdc, sc in next sc, (tr in next tr, sc in next sc) across to last 2 sts, work BPdc around post of next FPdc, dc in last dc.

Repeat Rows 3-8 for pattern until Panel measures approximately 50½", ending by working Row 8.

Last Row: Ch 3, turn; work FPdc around post of next BPdc, dc in each st across to last 2 sts, work FPdc around post of next BPdc, dc in last dc; finish off.

DIAMOND PANEL (Make 2)

Ch 18 **loosely**.

Row 1: Dc in fourth ch from hook and in each ch across: 16 sts.

Row 2 (Right side): Ch 3 **(counts as first dc, now and throughout)**, turn; work FPtr around post of next dc **(Fig. 1, page 1)**, dc in next 4 dc, work FPtr around post of next 4 dc, dc in next 4 dc, work FPtr around post of next dc, dc in last dc.

Note: Loop a short piece of yarn around any stitch to mark last row as **right** side.

Row 3: Ch 3, turn; work BPtr around post of next FPtr, dc in next 3 dc, skip next dc, work BPtr around post of next 2 FPtr, dc in same st as last BPtr and in next st, work BPtr around post of same FPtr as last dc and around post of next FPtr, skip next dc, dc in next 3 dc, work BPtr around post of next FPtr, dc in last dc.

Row 4: Ch 3, turn; work FPtr around post of next BPtr, dc in next 2 dc, skip next dc, work FPtr around post of next 2 BPtr, dc in same st as last FPtr and in next 3 sts, work FPtr around post of same BPtr as last dc and around post of next BPtr, skip next dc, dc in next 2 dc, work FPtr around post of next BPtr, dc in last dc.

Row 5: Ch 3, turn; work BPtr around post of next FPtr, dc in next dc, skip next dc, work BPtr around post of next 2 FPtr, dc in same st as last BPtr and in next 5 sts, work BPtr around post of same FPtr as last dc and around post of next FPtr, skip next dc, dc in next dc, work BPtr around post of next FPtr, dc in last dc.

Row 6: Ch 3, turn; work FPtr around post of next BPtr, dc in next 2 sts, work FPtr around post of same BPtr as last dc and around post of next BPtr, skip next dc, dc in next 4 dc, skip next dc, work FPtr around post of next 2 BPtr, dc in same st as last FPtr and in next dc, work FPtr around post of next BPtr, dc in last dc.

Row 7: Ch 3, turn; work BPtr around post of next FPtr, dc in next 3 sts, work BPtr around post of same FPtr as last dc and around post of next FPtr, skip next dc, dc in next 2 dc, skip next dc, work BPtr around post of next 2 FPtr, dc in same st as last BPtr and in next 2 dc, work BPtr around post of next FPtr, dc in last dc.

Row 8: Ch 3, turn; work FPtr around post of next BPtr, dc in next 4 sts, work FPtr around post of same BPtr as last dc and around post of next BPtr, skip next 2 dc, work FPtr around post of next 2 BPtr, dc in same st as last FPtr and in next 3 dc, work FPtr around post of next BPtr, dc in last dc.

Row 9: Ch 3, turn; work BPtr around post of next FPtr, dc in next 4 dc, skip next 2 FPtr, work BPtr around post of next 2 FPtr, working **behind** BPtr just made, work BPtr around post of first skipped FPtr and around post of next FPtr, dc in next 4 dc, work BPtr around post of next FPtr, dc in last dc.

Row 10: Ch 3, turn; work FPtr around post of next BPtr, dc in next 3 dc, skip next dc, work FPtr around post of next 2 BPtr, dc in same st as last FPtr and in next st, work FPtr around post of same BPtr as last dc and around post of next BPtr, skip next dc, dc in next 3 dc, work FPtr around post of next BPtr, dc in last dc.

Row 11: Ch 3, turn; work BPtr around post of next FPtr, dc in next 2 dc, skip next dc, work BPtr around post of next 2 FPtr, dc in same st as last BPtr and in next 3 sts, work BPtr around post of same FPtr as last dc and around post of next FPtr, skip next dc, dc in next 2 dc, work BPtr around post of next FPtr, dc in last dc.

Row 12: Ch 3, turn; work FPtr around post of next BPtr, dc in next dc, skip next dc, work FPtr around post of next 2 BPtr, dc in same st as last FPtr and in next 5 sts, work FPtr around post of same BPtr as last dc and around post of next BPtr, skip next dc, dc in next dc, work FPtr around post of next BPtr, dc in last dc.

Row 13: Ch 3, turn; work BPtr around post of next FPtr, dc in next 2 sts, work BPtr around post of same FPtr as last dc and around post of next FPtr, skip next dc, dc in next 4 dc, skip next dc, work BPtr around post of next 2 FPtr, dc in same st as last BPtr and in next dc, work BPtr around post of next FPtr, dc in last dc.

Row 14: Ch 3, turn; work FPtr around post of next BPtr, dc in next 3 sts, work FPtr around post of same BPtr as last dc and around post of next FPtr, skip next dc, dc in next 2 dc, skip next dc, work FPtr around post of next 2 BPtr, dc in same st as last FPtr and in next 2 dc, work FPtr around post of next BPtr, dc in last dc.

Row 15: Ch 3, turn; work BPtr around post of next FPtr, dc in next 4 sts, work BPtr around post of same FPtr as last dc and around post of next FPtr, skip next 2 dc, work BPtr around post of next 2 FPtr, dc in same st as last BPtr and in next 3 dc, work BPtr around post of next FPtr, dc in last dc.

Row 16: Ch 3, turn; work FPtr around post of next BPtr, dc in next 4 dc, skip next 2 BPtr, work FPtr around post of next 2 BPtr, working in **front** of FPtr just made, work FPtr around post of first skipped BPtr and around post of next BPtr, dc in next 4 dc, work FPtr around post of next BPtr, dc in last dc.
Repeat Rows 3-16 for pattern until Panel measures approximately 51″, ending by working Row 16.
Finish off.

CABLE PANEL (Make 2)

Ch 11 **loosely**.

Row 1 (Right side): Dc in fourth ch from hook and in each ch across: 9 sts.

Note: Loop a short piece of yarn around any stitch to mark last row as **right** side.

Row 2: Ch 3 **(counts as first dc, now and throughout)**, turn; work BPtr around post of next dc **(Fig. 1, page 1)**, dc in next 5 dc, work BPtr around post of next dc, dc in last dc.

Row 3: Ch 3, turn; work FPtr around post of next BPtr, dc in next 3 dc, work Cable as follows: ch 5 **loosely**, slip st from the front around post of dc 2 rows **below** same st (center dc) **(Fig. 4a)**, turn, hdc in each ch just completed **(Fig. 4b, Cable made)**, dc in next 2 dc, work FPtr around post of next BPtr, dc in last dc.

Fig. 4a

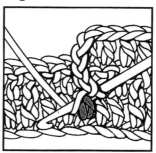

Fig. 4b

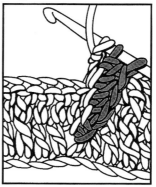

Row 4: Ch 3, turn; work BPtr around post of next FPtr, dc in next 5 dc, work BPtr around post of next FPtr, dc in last dc.

Row 5: Ch 3, turn; work FPtr around post of next BPtr, dc in next 3 dc, working to **right** of previous Cable, work Cable around post of dc 2 rows below **(Fig. 5)**, dc in next 2 dc, work FPtr around post of next BPtr, dc in last dc.
Repeat Rows 4 and 5 for pattern until Panel measures approximately 51″, ending by working Row 4.
Finish off.

Fig. 5

Continued on page 5.

POPCORN PANEL

Ch 35 **loosely**.

Row 1: Dc in fourth ch from hook and in each ch across: 33 sts.

Row 2 (Right side): Ch 3 **(counts as first dc, now and throughout)**, turn; work FPtr around post of next dc *(Fig. 1, page 1)*, dc in next 5 dc, ★ work Popcorn as follows: 5 dc in next dc, drop loop from hook, insert hook in first dc of 5-dc group, hook dropped loop and draw through *(Fig. 6, Popcorn made)*, dc in next 5 dc; repeat from ★ across to last 2 sts, work FPtr around post of next dc, dc in last dc: 4 Popcorns.

Note: Loop a short piece of yarn around any stitch to mark last row as **right** side.

Row 3 AND ALL WRONG SIDE ROWS: Ch 3, turn; work BPtr around post of next FPtr *(Fig. 1, page 1)*, dc in next st and in each st across to last 2 sts, work BPtr around post of next FPtr, dc in last dc.

Row 4: Ch 3, turn; work FPtr around post of next BPtr, dc in next 2 dc, work Popcorn, (dc in next 5 dc, work Popcorn) across to last 4 sts, dc in next 2 dc, work FPtr around post of next BPtr, dc in last dc: 5 Popcorns.

Row 6: Ch 3, turn; work FPtr around post of next BPtr, dc in next 5 dc, (work Popcorn, dc in next 5 dc) across to last 2 sts, work FPtr around post of next BPtr, dc in last dc: 4 Popcorns.

Repeat Rows 3-6 for pattern until Panel measures approximately 51″, ending by working Row 3.

Finish off.

Fig. 6

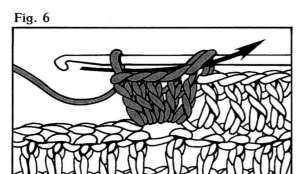

JOINING

Lay out Panels using Chart as a guide for placement [being sure that the beginning chain or bottom edge of each Panel (Row 1) is at the same end].

With **right** sides of 2 Panels facing you, hold edges together. Catch one strand from each edge, being careful to match rows *(Fig. 7)*.

Join remaining Panels in same manner.

Fig. 7

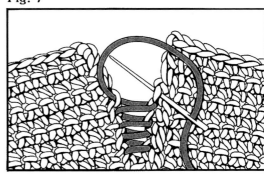

EDGING

With **right** side facing, join yarn with slip st in end of first row; ch 1, working in end of rows, sc evenly across.

Repeat for second side.

Using three strands of yarn, attach Fringe in every other stitch across each end of Afghan *(Figs. 2a & b, page 1)*.

CHART

Twist Panel
Bobble Panel
Diamond Panel
Cable Panel
Popcorn Panel
Cable Panel
Diamond Panel
Bobble Panel
Twist Panel

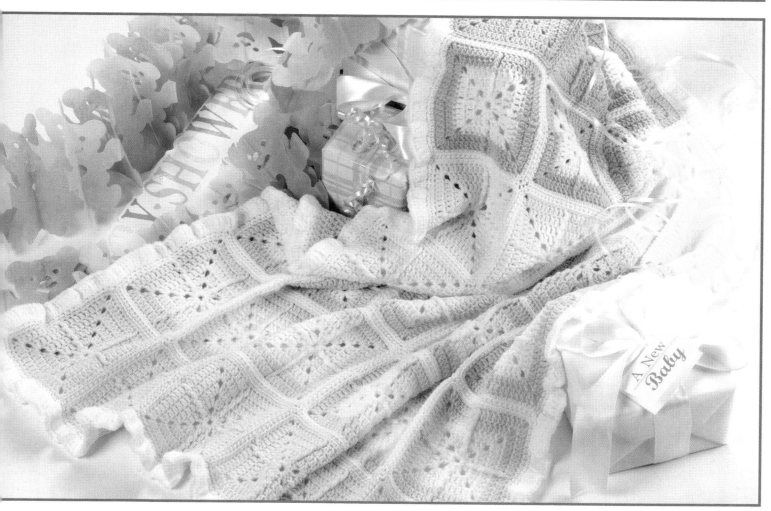

Spiderweb

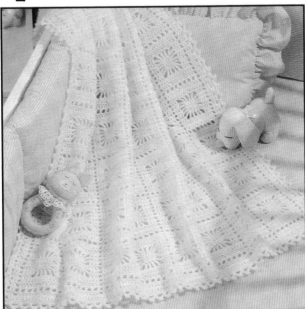

Finished Size: Approximately 34¼" x 46½"

MATERIALS

Sport Weight Yarn, approximately:
13 ounces, (370 grams, 1,255 yards)
Crochet hook, size G (4.50 mm) **or** size needed for gauge

GAUGE: 16 dc and 10 rows = 4"

Ch 137 **loosely**.
Row 1: Dc in fourth ch from hook and in each ch across:135 sts.
Row 2 (Right side): Ch 3 **(counts as first dc, now and throughout)**, turn; dc in next 2 dc, ch 1, skip next dc, ★ dc in next 15 dc, ch 1, skip next dc; repeat from ★ across to last 3 dc, dc in last 3 dc.
Note: Loop a short piece of yarn around any stitch to mark last row as **right** side.
Row 3: Ch 3, turn; dc in next 2 dc, ch 1, ★ dc in next dc, (ch 1, skip next dc, dc in next dc) 7 times, ch 1; repeat from ★ across to last 3 dc, dc in last 3 dc.
Row 4: Ch 3, turn; dc in next 2 dc, ch 1, ★ dc in next dc, (dc in next ch-1 sp, dc in next dc) 7 times, ch 1; repeat from ★ across to last 3 dc, dc in last 3 dc.
Row 5: Ch 3, turn; dc in next 2 dc, ch 1, ★ dc in next 15 dc, ch 1; repeat from ★ across to last 3 dc, dc in last 3 dc.
Row 6: Ch 3, turn; dc in next 2 dc, ch 1, ★ dc in next 3 dc, ch 3, skip next dc, (tr in next dc, skip next dc) 4 times, ch 3, dc in next 3 dc, ch 1; repeat from ★ across to last 3 dc, dc in last 3 dc.
Row 7: Ch 3, turn; dc in next 2 dc, ch 1, ★ dc in next 3 dc, ch 3, sc in next 4 tr, ch 3, dc in next 3 dc, ch 1; repeat from ★ across to last 3 dc, dc in last 3 dc.
Rows 8-10: Ch 3, turn; dc in next 2 dc, ch 1, ★ dc in next 3 dc, ch 3, sc in next 4 sc, ch 3, dc in next 3 dc, ch 1; repeat from ★ across to last 3 dc, dc in last 3 dc.
Row 11: Ch 3, turn; dc in next 2 dc, ch 1, ★ dc in next 3 dc, ch 1, (tr in next sc, ch 1) 4 times, dc in next 3 dc, ch 1; repeat from ★ across to last 3 dc, dc in last 3 dc.
Row 12: Ch 3, turn; dc in next 2 dc, ch 1, ★ dc in next 3 dc, dc in next ch-1 sp, (dc in next tr, dc in next ch-1 sp) 4 times, dc in next 3 dc, ch 1; repeat from ★ across to last 3 dc, dc in last 3 dc.
Row 13: Repeat Row 5.
Rows 14-114: Repeat Rows 3-13, 9 times; then repeat Rows 3 and 4 once **more**.
Row 115: Ch 3, turn; dc in each dc and in each ch-1 sp across.

EDGING

Rnd 1: Ch 1, turn; work 136 sc evenly spaced across last row; working in end of rows, 3 sc in first row, work 173 sc evenly spaced across to last row, 3 sc in last row; working in free loops of beginning ch, work 136 sc evenly spaced across; working in end of rows, 3 sc in first row, work 173 sc evenly spaced across to last row, 3 sc in last row; join with slip st to first sc: 630 sc.
Rnd 2: Ch 1, ★ sc in next sc, ch 4, sc in third ch from hook, ch 2, skip next 2 sc; repeat from ★ around; join with slip st to first sc, finish off.

Ripples

Finished Size: Approximately 38½" x 52"

MATERIALS

Sport Weight Yarn, approximately:
20 ounces, (570 grams, 2,000 yards)
Crochet hook, size G (4.50 mm) **or** size needed for gauge

GAUGE: 16 hdc and 12 rows = 4"

Ch 155 **loosely**.
Row 1 (Right side): Hdc in third ch from hook and in each ch across: 154 sts.
Note: Loop a short piece of yarn around any stitch to mark last row as **right** side.
Row 2: Ch 2 **(counts as first hdc, now and throughout)**, turn; hdc in next 8 hdc, [YO and pull up a loop in next hdc, skip next hdc, YO and pull up a loop in next hdc, YO and draw through all 5 loops on hook **(Fig. 8, hdc decrease made)**], ★ hdc in next 7 hdc, 2 hdc in each of next 2 hdc, hdc in next 7 hdc, work hdc decrease; repeat from ★ across to last 9 hdc, hdc in last 9 hdc: 152 hdc.

Fig. 8

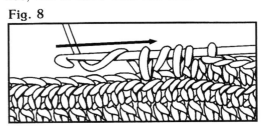

11

Row 3: Ch 2, turn; hdc in next hdc and in each hdc across.
Row 4: Ch 5 (**counts as first tr plus ch 1**), turn; (tr, ch 1) twice in same st, ★ † skip next hdc, (tr in next hdc, skip next hdc) 3 times, [YO twice, pull up a loop in next hdc, (YO and draw through 2 loops on hook) twice, skip next hdc, YO twice, pull up a loop in next hdc, (YO and draw through 2 loops on hook) twice, YO and draw through all 3 loops on hook (**Fig. 9, tr decrease made**)], skip next hdc, (tr in next hdc, skip next hdc) 3 times, (ch 1, tr) 3 times in next hdc †, (tr, ch 1) twice in next hdc; repeat from ★ 6 times **more**, then repeat from † to † once.
Row 5: Ch 2, turn; hdc in first tr and in each ch and tr across to last tr, 2 hdc in last tr: 154 hdc.
Repeat Rows 2-5 for pattern until Afghan measures approximately 52″, ending by working Row 3.
Finish off.

Fig. 9

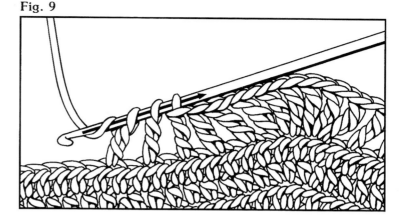

Basketweave

Finished Size: Approximately 33½″ x 46½″

MATERIALS
Sport Weight Yarn, approximately:
  32 ounces, (910 grams, 3,200 yards)
Crochet hook, size F (4.00 mm) **or** size needed for gauge

GAUGE: 20 Post Sts and 15 rows = 4″

Ch 158 **loosely**.
Row 1: Dc in fourth ch from hook and in each ch across: 156 sts.
Row 2 (Right side): Ch 2, turn; work Front Post dc (**abbreviated FPdc**) around post of next 14 sts (**Fig. 1, page 1**), ★ work Back Post dc (**abbreviated BPdc**) around post of next 14 sts, work FPdc around post of next 14 sts; repeat from ★ across to last st, hdc in top of turning ch.
Note: Loop a short piece of yarn around any stitch to mark last row as **right** side.
Row 3: Ch 2, turn; work BPdc around post of next 14 sts, ★ work FPdc around post of next 14 sts, work BPdc around post of next 14 sts; repeat from ★ across to last st, hdc in top of turning ch.
Rows 4-11: Repeat Rows 2 and 3, 4 times.
Row 12: Repeat Row 3.
Rows 13-22: Repeat Rows 2 and 3, 5 times.
Row 23: Repeat Row 3.
Rows 24-165: Repeat Rows 2-23, 6 times; then repeat Rows 2-11 once **more**.
EDGING
Rnd 1: Ch 1, turn; work 153 sc evenly spaced across last row; working in end of rows, 3 sc in end of first row, work 201 sc evenly spaced across to last row, 3 sc in last row; working in free loops of beginning ch, work 153 sc evenly spaced across; working in end of rows, 3 sc in end of first row, work 201 sc evenly spaced across to last row, 3 sc in last row; join with slip st to first sc: 720 sc.
Rnd 2: Slip st in next sc, ch 4 (**counts as first dc plus ch 1**), (skip next sc, dc in next sc, ch 1) 76 times, † (dc, ch 1) 3 times in next sc, dc in next sc, ch 1, (skip next sc, dc in next sc, ch 1) 101 times, (dc, ch 1) 3 times in next sc, dc in next sc, ch 1 †, (skip next sc, dc in next sc, ch 1) 77 times, repeat from † to † once; join with slip st to first dc: 744 sts.
Rnd 3: Slip st in first ch-1 sp and in next dc, ch 5 (**counts as first tr plus ch 1**), [tr, (ch 1, tr) 3 times] in same dc, skip next dc, sc in next dc, ★ skip next dc, [tr, (ch 1, tr) 4 times] in next dc, skip next dc, sc in next dc; repeat from ★ around; join with slip st to first tr.
Rnd 4: ★ Slip st in ch-1 sp and in next tr, [ch 3, slip st in third ch from hook (**Picot made**)], slip st in next ch-1 sp, (work Picot, slip st in next tr and in next ch-1 sp) twice, slip st in next 3 sts; repeat from ★ around; join with slip st to first st, finish off.

Stripes

Finished Size: Approximately 29½" x 39¼"

MATERIALS
Sport Weight Yarn, approximately:
  Main Color: 8½ ounces, (240 grams, 1,065 yards)
  Color A: 1½ ounces, (40 grams, 190 yards)
  Color B: 1½ ounces, (40 grams, 190 yards)
Crochet hook, size G (4.50 mm) **or** size needed for gauge

GAUGE: In pattern, 16 sts and 16 rows = 4"

Note: Afghan is worked from side to side.

STRIPE SEQUENCE
14 Rows Main Color, ★ 2 rows Color A, 2 rows Main Color, 4 rows Color B, 2 rows Main Color, 2 rows Color A, 14 rows Main Color; repeat from ★ for sequence.

With Main Color, ch 158 **loosely**.
Row 1 (Right side): Insert hook and pull up a loop in second and third chs from hook, YO and draw through all 3 loops on hook, ch 1, ★ (insert hook in next ch and pull up a loop) twice, YO and draw through all 3 loops on hook, ch 1; repeat from ★ across to last ch, sc in last ch: 157 sts.
Note: Loop a short piece of yarn around any stitch to mark last row as **right** side.
Row 2: Ch 1, turn; insert hook and pull up a loop in first sc and in first ch-1 sp, YO and draw through all 3 loops on hook, ch 1, ★ insert hook and pull up a loop in next st and in next ch-1 sp, YO and draw through all 3 loops on hook, ch 1; repeat from ★ across to last st, sc in last st.
Repeat Row 2 in Stripe Sequence until Afghan measures approximately 29½", ending by working 14 rows of Main Color. Finish off.

Using three strands of yarn and matching colors, attach Fringe in every other row across each end of Afghan *(Figs. 2a & b, page 1)*.

Zig Zag Filet

Finished Size: Approximately 31½" x 41½"

MATERIALS
Sport Weight Yarn, approximately:
  17 ounces, (480 grams, 1,700 yards)
Crochet hook, size G (4.50 mm) **or** size needed for gauge

GAUGE: 14 dc and 8 rows = 4"

Note: Afghan is worked from side to side.

Ch 147 **loosely**.
Row 1 (Right side): Dc in fourth ch from hook and in each ch across: 145 sts.
Note: Loop a short piece of yarn around any stitch to mark last row as **right** side.
Row 2: Ch 4 (**counts as first dc plus ch 1, now and throughout**), turn; skip next dc, ★ dc in next 10 dc, ch 1, skip next dc; repeat from ★ across to last 11 dc, dc in last 11 dc.
Row 3: Ch 3 (**counts as first dc, now and throughout**), turn; ★ dc in next 8 dc, ch 1, skip next dc, dc in next dc, dc in next ch-1 sp; repeat from ★ across to last dc, dc in last dc.
Row 4: Ch 3, turn; dc in next 2 dc, dc in next ch-1 sp, dc in next dc, ch 1, skip next dc, ★ dc in next 8 dc, dc in next ch-1 sp, dc in next dc, ch 1, skip next dc; repeat from ★ across to last 7 dc, dc in last 7 dc.
Row 5: Ch 3, turn; dc in next 4 dc, ch 1, skip next dc, dc in next dc, dc in next ch-1 sp, ★ dc in next 8 dc, ch 1, skip next dc, dc in next dc, dc in next ch-1 sp; repeat from ★ across to last 5 dc, dc in last 5 dc.
Row 6: Ch 3, turn; dc in next 6 dc, dc in next ch-1 sp, dc in next dc, ch 1, skip next dc, ★ dc in next 8 dc, dc in next ch-1 sp, dc in next dc, ch 1, skip next dc; repeat from ★ across to last 3 dc, dc in last 3 dc.
Row 7: Ch 4, turn; skip next dc, dc in next dc, dc in next ch-1 sp, ★ dc in next 8 dc, ch 1, skip next dc, dc in next dc, dc in next ch-1 sp; repeat from ★ across to last 9 dc, dc in last 9 dc.
Rows 8-62: Repeat Rows 3-7, 11 times.
Row 63: Ch 3, turn; dc in next dc and in each dc and ch-1 sp across.

EDGING: Ch 1, working in end of rows, sc evenly across first edge (Top) of Afghan; finish off.

Using three strands of yarn, attach Fringe in space between every other dc across each side and in every row across bottom *(Figs. 2a & b, page 1)*.

13